CHILDREN'S AND YOUNG ADULTS
BOOK EXAMINATION CENTER
MISSOURI STATE LIBRARY

BLIZZARD
at the Zoo

BLIZZARD at the Zoo

by Robert Bahr
pictures by Consuelo Joerns

Lothrop, Lee & Shepard Books   New York

Readers may be interested to know the identities of the following animals, not specifically mentioned in the text: gorilla, p. 6; greater kudu and crowned crane, p. 7; elk, p. 8; Syrian brown bear, p. 9; mallard duck, canvas-back duck, bufflehead duck, red-breasted merganser duck, p. 10; mallard ducks, mute swan, Canada goose, p. 11; pair of troupials (or bugle birds), double-collared aracari (a type of toucan), Java sparrow (on the wing), masked lovebird, p. 20; Canada duck, pintail ducks (foreground), mute swan, canvas-back duck, mallard (farthest back), p. 27.

The jacket front shows a toucan, giraffe, buffalo, gibbon monkey, and a zebra, while the back shows a California sea lion, gorilla, mallard duck, and a polar bear.

Text copyright © 1982 by Robert Bahr. Illustrations copyright © 1982 by Consuelo Joerns. All rights reserved. No part of this book may be reproduced or utilized in any form or by any means, electronic or mechanical, including photocopying, recording or by any information storage and retrieval system, without permission in writing from the Publisher. Inquiries should be addressed to Lothrop, Lee & Shepard Books, a division of William Morrow & Company, Inc., 105 Madison Avenue, New York, New York 10016. Printed in the United States of America. First Edition. 1 2 3 4 5 6 7 8 9 10

Library of Congress Cataloging in Publication Data. Bahr, Robert. Blizzard at the zoo. Summary: Relates the efforts to keep the animals of the Buffalo Zoo alive and fed during the first day of the blizzard of 1977, one of the worst in American history. 1. Buffalo Zoo—Juvenile literature. 2. Buffalo—Blizzard, 1977—Juvenile literature. [1. Buffalo Zoo. 2. Zoological gardens. 3. Buffalo—Blizzard, 1977. 4. Blizzards] I. Joerns, Consuelo. II. Title. QL76.5.U62B832   590'.74'474797   80-22285   AACR1 ISBN 0-688-00423-7   ISBN 0-688-00424-5 (lib. bdg.)

TO MY SON,
JAMES DAVID

With grateful thanks to
Gerald D. Aquilina,
Curator of Mammals at the Buffalo Zoo,
for his assistance.

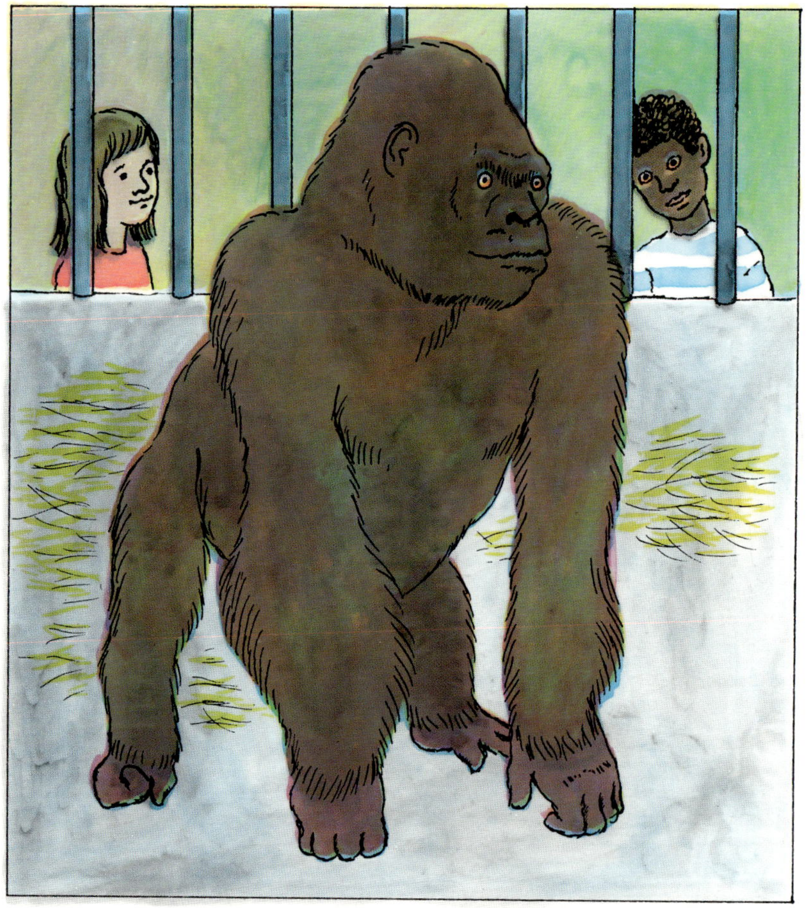

You know what a zoo is like in the summer—a friendly place where you can see all kinds of animals and birds.

Have you ever wondered what happens in winter?

This true story tells you what happened in 1977 at the zoo in Buffalo, New York.

On January 28, as the animal keepers made their rounds, the sky grew strangely dark. The temperature dropped more than thirty degrees—to well below freezing—in less than ten minutes. Suddenly snow fell thick and fast. The wind whipped it around in big, white, ever-changing drifts.

Ducks, and swans, and geese were getting trapped in their pond as the water started to freeze. Ice was forming on their wings. They couldn't fly in the snow and wind, and they would die if they weren't rescued. Keepers struggled to reach the pond. Emergency supplies were piled into the zoo's van.

The ducks closest to shore were saved as the van churned through the snow from the main building. As soon as it arrived, the birds were rushed inside and wrapped in towels. The keepers working in the van held one, two, or even three birds under their jackets, to warm them gradually. If they had warmed the waterfowl more quickly, the birds would have died of shock.

The pond was freezing rapidly, but the ice was still too thin to walk across. The birds huddled on the island in the middle of the pond were trapped. The keepers had to use long-handled nets, from the van, to scoop birds off the snow. This took patience and careful aim. The blowing snow made the job even more difficult. Sometimes it was impossible to see across the water.

Once a keeper thought she'd rescued a swan. Instead, she found a clump of ice in her hands.

Finally, after two hours, the last bird to be found was lifted to safety. Then the van churned through the snow again, taking over forty birds to the children's zoo barn.

As the hours passed, the elk stayed outside, untroubled by the snow and freezing winds.

Polar bears love the cold. Slow moving in summer, they now played together, romping and wrestling, sliding on the ice and diving into their pool.

The thick-pelted buffalo hadn't moved since the storm started. The weatherman had predicted a few snow flurries, followed by clearing skies, but now the buffalo were covered on top by blankets of snow. It actually kept them warm! The steam from their nostrils rose like the smoke of many fires, creating openings in the snow so that they could breathe.

It was still snowing when the keepers went home for the evening.

The three California sea lions had a holiday that night. How they barked! They played so vigorously in their pond that the water couldn't freeze, even in the sub-zero weather.

It was snowing more lightly now, but tons and tons of snow were moving. The wind blew them into the zoo from the golf course across the street. Finally, the zoo's eight-foot-high fence disappeared under a mountain of snow.

The next morning, the city of Buffalo was like a ghost town. There were thousands of cars, but none were moving. Throughout the night, drivers had abandoned them to seek shelter. The cars were scattered in every direction, stuck, and often buried, in the snow. There was no public transportation, and driving conditions were too dangerous. The wind blowing the snow made it impossible to see. (There was zero visibility.) Only eight keepers were able to get through the storm to the zoo.

The polar bears were found testing the snow that filled the moat surrounding their area, patting it with their huge front paws. These polar bears each weighed over one thousand pounds. Careful by nature, they wanted to be sure that the snow would support their weight before they tried to walk across the moat. Such caution had served them well in the Arctic, where they'd been born. One mistake there and a bear could easily fall beneath snow-covered ice, get trapped, and drown. Here, they could fall to the bottom of the moat. Luckily, their keeper was able to lure them, with food, to their shelter.

There was no real problem feeding the animals who lived in the main building. The green snake and the crocodile had been fed before the blizzard. Like other reptiles, they could go without eating for another few weeks, if necessary.

The lions, and the tiger, need vitamins and eight to ten pounds of horsemeat daily. The horsemeat was kept in the main building kitchen, the vitamins nearby.

None of the big cats had to roar for food.

The small tropical birds needed plenty of seeds, sugar water, fruit, vegetables, and mealworms. Many of these birds eat nonstop all day long, to keep up their energy. There was plenty of food for them in the kitchen, too.

The blizzard did inconvenience this baboon, a mandrill. His favorite fruits and vegetables were usually delivered, fresh, to the zoo several times a week. Hardly anyone could drive in the blinding winds, so the mandrill had to make do with monkey chow.

The giraffes were warm indoors—but their house was far away from the main building. Huge snowdrifts had to be cleared away before their keeper could reach them.

Other keepers gave bales of timothy hay and pounds of grain to the zebras. Though native to Africa, these hardy animals don't mind snow.

The donkeys and ponies who lived in the children's zoo needed food that morning.

So did the waterfowl, who were surviving nicely in the children's zoo barn.

And, of course, Mamie, the Indian elephant, demanded her fair share of food–and attention.

The black buck antelope and the camel came out of their shelters to wait.

Don't forget the bald eagles!
These large outdoor birds like fish.

The keepers worked hard, shoveling paths to each animal. When a food storage area was buried under the snow, they delivered meals on toboggans and sleds loaned to them by people from the neighborhood.

While the keepers worked, the sea lions slapped the water with their flippers and barked without stopping. They made so much noise that they could be heard even above the howling of the wind.

   Then, as one keeper dumped forty pounds of mackerel into their water (which never did freeze because the sea lions kept it stirred up so), the barking stopped. The sea lions swallowed the long, shiny fish in great gulps, bumping each other out of the way to get at the food.

Even the buffalo, who played in the snow, frisking and tossing great piles of it about with their heads, had been fed by the animal keepers.

It was time to go home.